eXTREME SPORTS BIOGRAPHIES™

TONY HAWK

Skateboarding Champion

Ian F. Mahaney

The Rosen Publishing Group's

PowerKids Press™

New York

To my wife, Jenet. Someday you'll land that Kickflip McTwist!

Safety gear, including helmets, wrist guards, kneepads, and elbow pads should be worn while skateboarding. Do not attempt tricks without proper gear, instruction, and supervision.

Published in 2005 by The Rosen Publishing Group, Inc.
29 East 21st Street, New York, NY 10010

Copyright © 2005 by The Rosen Publishing Group, Inc.

First Edition

Editor: Heidi Leigh Johansen
Book Design: Mike Donnellan
Photo Researcher: Peter Tomlinson

Photo Credits: Cover, pp. 4, 8, 11 Robert Beck/Icon SMI; p. 4 (inset) © *Thrasher* magazine; p. 7 © John Storey/Time Life Pictures/Getty Images; p. 12 © Richard Mackson/Time Life Pictures/Getty Images; pp. 12 (inset), 15 Icon Sports Media; p. 16 Shelly Castellano/Icon SMI; pp. 16 (inset), 20 Getty Images; p. 19 Tony Donaldson/Icon SMI; p. 22 © Kathy Hutchins/Hutchins Photo.

Library of Congress Cataloging-in-Publication Data

Mahaney, Ian F.
Tony Hawk : skateboarding champion / Ian F. Mahaney.— 1st ed.
    p. cm. — (Extreme sports biographies)
Summary: A biography of the professional skateboarder who performed the first "900" at the X Games in 1999, invented numerous skateboarding moves, and helped revive the popularity of this sport.
Includes bibliographical references (p.).
ISBN 1-4042-2747-4 (Library Binding)
1. Hawk, Tony—Juvenile literature. 2. Skateboarders—United States—Biography—Juvenile literature. [1. Hawk, Tony. 2. Skateboarders.] I. Title. II. Series.
GV859.813.H39M35 2005
796.22'092—dc22

2003022058

Manufactured in the United States of America

Contents

Skateboarding started about 100 years ago, when kids attached steel roller-skate wheels to spare pieces of wood. Today riders like Tony Hawk, shown here in two early photos as a young skater, ride skateboards with plastic wheels.

Extreme Skateboarding

Skateboarding is a popular **extreme sport**. In skateboarding, or skating, as many people call it, a rider balances on a wooden board called a deck. The deck sits on four small wheels. Skateboard decks are from 7 to 10 inches (18–25 cm) wide and about 2 ½ feet (.8 m) long. Decks are covered with **grip tape** to hold riders' shoes firmly on the skateboard. Today skateboard wheels are made of a hard plastic. Many people think that skateboarding is not a safe sport. However, it can be a safe, enjoyable sport, as long as you skateboard in a place that is meant for skateboarding, such as a **skate park**. You must also wear safety gear, including kneepads, elbow pads, wrist guards, and a helmet. Tony Hawk is one of the best-known **professional** skateboarders in the world. Tony has helped to make skateboarding a popular and **mainstream** sport.

Tony Hawk is a very accomplished skateboarding **champion**. Tony was born on May 12, 1968, in San Diego, California. Tony's parents' names are Frank and Nancy Hawk. Tony has two older sisters, Pat and Lenore, and an older brother, Steve. When Tony was nine years old, Steve lent Tony a blue **fiberglass** skateboard. The skateboard was called a banana board and was much skinnier than today's skateboards. Tony had played other sports, but none satisfied him as much as skateboarding did. Tony was not skating for money or for fame. He was just having a great time! Tony skated on the sidewalks of his neighborhood in Tierrasanta, California. Tony's father, Frank, **encouraged** Tony's love for skating. Later, Frank Hawk even started two skateboard **leagues**, including the National Skateboard Association (NSA), to advance the sport of skateboarding.

Frank and Tony share a skateboarding moment. Frank Hawk died in 1995, but his work lives on. The National Skateboard Association established skateboarding guidelines and provided safety tips that are still used today.

Tony flies through the air while pulling the board away from his feet with one hand. Skateboarding tricks can consist of ollies to "catch air," twists on the board, and spins in midair. Many skateboarders perform tricks off railings, steps, curbs, and other objects. Some even skate in empty swimming pools!

Tony's First Tricks

Steve Hawk taught Tony how to balance on a skateboard. Soon Tony learned how to **perform** tricks, such as an ollie. An ollie is a trick in which the rider pushes down hard on the back of the board so that the deck bounces up into the air with the rider on it. Tony mastered many basic tricks. Soon Tony started reading *Skateboarder* magazine, which **inspired** him to push himself as a skateboarder. Tony practiced at a skate park near his home, called the Oasis. At age 11, Tony entered his first skateboarding **competition** at the Oasis. Tony did not do well. In fact, he fell several times. His failure made him more **determined**. Tony worked hard every day on **complex** tricks and moves. Tony caught the attention of a skateboard company called Dogtown, which offered to **sponsor** him. Dogtown gave Tony free gear and paid for him to enter skateboarding competitions.

Tony Joins the Bones Brigade

Tony Hawk skated often at the Del Mar Surf and Turf, a top skate park near San Diego, where the best skaters in the area skated. A skater named Stacy Peralta saw Tony skateboarding in a competition there. Peralta invited Tony to join his skateboard team, called the Bones Brigade. The Bones Brigade was a group of skaters that toured, competed, and made skating videos. Tony had the opportunity to skate with some of the world's best skaters, including Rodney Mullen, Steve Caballero, and Mike McGill. Tony was only 12 years old, though, and he was a very thin boy. Tony's small size made it **difficult** for him to perform many of the tricks that the bigger skaters could perform. So Tony did what any normal kid would do. He invented his own tricks and new ways to catch air. People loved to watch him skateboard because he was so small, yet he was so fast and daring.

Tony catches air as a teenage skater. To perform midair tricks, most skaters use their body weight to gain speed. As a young skater, Tony could not do that because he was small and did not have enough body weight to make the skateboard go fast. Instead, Tony invented new ways to catch air and to go fast.

Tony pulls a daring move at a skate park. Even a professional can get hurt! Tony has hurt himself many times. He has suffered from a broken elbow, sprained ankles, and broken front teeth. Tony has also had surgery on his knee. Inset: Tony puts on all of his safety gear before a competition.

Tony Turns Pro

For the next two years, Tony Hawk skated with the Bones Brigade as an **amateur**. After school, Tony spent all of his free time skateboarding. At age 14, Tony turned professional, or pro. Being a professional skateboarder was a way for Tony to continue doing what he loved best. Tony's family moved to Cardiff, California, and Tony started high school. Tony practiced skating at the nearby skate park, the Del Mar Surf and Turf. He competed in National Skateboard Association events in the summer of 1983, and he toured the world with the Bones Brigade, traveling to Europe and Australia. Tony did so well in the NSA events that he finished in first place in the entire tour. Tony's hard work as a young skateboarder at the Oasis and as the youngest member of the Bones Brigade had paid off. Tony was only 15 years old and he was on top of the world!

The Best in the World

As Tony Hawk grew, he became stronger. Tony was able to perform extremely complex tricks and was still inventing new ones. Tony was skilled at skateboarding because he had been skating for so many years that he had become very comfortable on a board. He was also creative and worked hard. One of Tony's most famous moves was the 720, performed on the **half-pipe**. In a 720, Tony rides up the half-pipe and spins two complete times in the air before landing and riding down the half-pipe. In 1984, Tony won the NSA championship again, then again in 1985, and again in 1986. By the time Tony graduated from Torrey Pines High School in 1986, he was considered the best skater in the world. Skateboarding was becoming very popular, and so was Tony. He was even featured on the cover of magazines, including *Thrasher*.

Tony performs a 360 on the half-pipe. A 360 is spinning in a full circle, or 360 degrees, so a 720-degree spin is two complete spins and a 900 is two and one-half spins!

In 1990, Tony married his first wife, Cindy Dunbar. They had one son together, named Hudson Riley Hawk. Cindy and Tony separated when Riley was a child. Riley, shown here skating while Tony looks on, enjoys skateboarding as much as his father does. Inset: Tony's signature board was a huge success!

Success!

Tony Hawk began skating for fun. As a kid, he never thought he would become a famous professional skateboarder. Powell Peralta, the same company that offered Tony entrance to the Bones Brigade, sponsored Tony. Powell Peralta asked Tony to **design** a **signature board**. The Tony Hawk Signature Board sold hundreds of thousands of copies, which means that young skateboarders all over the world began using skateboards that Tony had designed and created! Tony performed in many skateboarding movies and acted in a movie with Christian Slater called *Gleaming the Cube*. Tony even appeared in ads for milk and for the soda Mountain Dew. Tony was doing what he loved to do most, and he was able to buy two houses near San Diego by the time he was 19 years old.

The X Games and the 900

Tony had become the superstar of skateboarding as a teenager. However, the sport went through a hard time from the late 1980s until the mid-1990s, because fewer skaters were interested in the sport. Tony and another skater, named Per Welinder, started a skating company called Birdhouse Projects. Birdhouse Projects made new deck designs and skateboarding gear. Skateboarding got more attention in 1995, when ESPN aired the Extreme Games, now called the X Games, on TV. This brought extreme sports to a wider group of people. The X Games is an extreme sports competition held every year. Tony's most famous X-Games moment came in 1999 in San Francisco, California. Tony completed a trick that many fans thought was impossible. He landed the first 900. In a 900, Tony spins two and one-half times in the air after jumping off the top of the half-pipe on his board.

Tony performs his fantastic 900 in the vert event at the 2003 X Games. Vert is a competition held on the half-pipe in which skaters perform as many cool tricks as possible. Tony came in first or second place every year from 1995 to 1999 in vert, starting with winning first place in 1995.

In an airwalk, Tony uses a railing, the edge of a half-pipe, or even a table to jump into the air on his skateboard. Then he removes both feet from the board, so that it looks as if he is walking on air. Tony invented the airwalk when he was 15 years old. No wonder Tony is called Birdman!

Birdman's Famous Moves

Tony's nickname is Birdman. Tony may be called Birdman because his last name is Hawk, like the **fierce** bird. Tony also may be called Birdman because he flies through the air performing outstanding tricks. Tony has invented between 50 and 100 skateboarding tricks. One of his famous tricks is called the stalefish. The story goes that this trick got its name while Tony was working at a summer skate camp in Sweden. Tony was practicing a new, difficult trick. Later, one of the young campers saw Tony write down the words "stale fish" to describe his lunch. The camper asked if that was the name of Tony's new trick. Since Tony hadn't named the trick yet, the name stalefish stuck. In a stalefish, Tony twists around in midair and **grabs** the board with his trailing, or back, hand. Other famous tricks Tony invented include the airwalk, the frontside cab revert, and the ollie 540.

Tony Hawk married Erin, his second wife, in 1996. Tony and Erin have two sons, named Spencer and Keegan Hawk. All three of Tony's children like to ride skateboards. Tony does not compete anymore, but he still skateboards every day. Sometimes he even shows up secretly at skate parks during the summer as a surprise to the young skaters! Tony is a proud father and spends much of his time with his kids. Through the Tony Hawk **Foundation**, Tony gives about $400,000 per year to communities around the country to help them pay for skate parks. Tony created Boom Boom HuckJam, an event that mixes extreme sports with popular music. Tony helped to produce two video games, called Tony Hawk's Pro Skater and Tony Hawk's Underground. If you practice hard and stay safe, one day you may be able to skate like Tony!

Glossary

amateur (A-muh-tur) Someone who lacks practice in something.

champion (CHAM-pee-un) The best, or the winner.

competition (kom-pih-TIH-shin) A game.

complex (kom-PLEKS) Very hard to do.

design (dih-ZYN) To plan the form of something.

determined (dih-TER-mind) Being very set on doing something.

difficult (DIH-fih-kult) Hard to do.

encouraged (in-KUR-ijd) To have filled with strength or to have offered help.

extreme sport (ek-STREEM SPORT) A bold and uncommon sport, such as BMX, in-line skating, motocross, skateboarding, snowboarding, and wakeboarding.

fiberglass (FY-ber-glas) A matter made of glass and other things.

fierce (FEERS) Strong and ready to fight.

foundation (fown-DAY-shun) A group that helps people.

grabs (GRABZ) Catches and holds with one's hand.

grip tape (GRIP TAYP) A sticky sandpaper.

half-pipe (HAF-pyp) A ramp that is shaped like a big *U*.

inspired (in-SPYRD) To have sparked or awakened feelings for something.

leagues (LEEGZ) Groups that run events.

mainstream (MAYN-streem) Popular or well-known.

perform (per-FORM) To carry out, to do.

professional (pruh-FEH-shuh-nul) Paid for what he or she does.

signature board (SIG-nuh-cher BORD) A special deck created by a skateboarder.

skate park (SKAYT PARK) A park for skaters.

sponsor (SPON-ser) To give gear and money to a sportsman or sportswoman.

Index

Web Sites

Due to the changing nature of Internet links, PowerKids Press has developed an online list of Web sites related to the subject of this book. This site is updated regularly. Please use this link to access the list: www.powerkidslinks.com/esb/hawk/

10/06